Ocean Food Chains

Emma Lynch

www.heinemann.co.uk/library
Visit our website to find out more information about Heinemann Library books.

To order:
 Phone 44 (0) 1865 888066
 Send a fax to 44 (0) 1865 314091
 Visit the Heinemann Bookshop at www.heinemann.co.uk/library to browse our catalogue and order online.

First published in Great Britain by Heinemann Library, Halley Court, Jordan Hill, Oxford OX2 8EJ, part of Harcourt Education. Heinemann is a registered trademark of Harcourt Education Ltd.

Editorial: Sarah Eason and Kathy Peltan
Design: Jo Hinton-Malivoire and AMR
Illustration: Words and Publications
Picture Research: Ruth Blair and Ginny Stroud-Lewis
Production: Camilla Smith

Originated by Ambassador Litho Ltd
Printed in China by WKT Company Limited.

The paper used to print this book comes from sustainable resources

ISBN 0 431 11902 3
09 08 07 06 05 04
10 9 8 7 6 5 4 3 2 1

British Library Cataloguing in Publication Data
Lynch, Emma
Food Chains: Oceans
577.7'16
A full catalogue record for this book is available from the British Library.

Acknowledgements
The Publishers would like to thank the following for permission to reproduce photographs: Alamy p. **27** (Mr Vivak Gour-Broome); Corbis pp. **14** (Peter Johnson), **19** (Galen Rowell), **23** (Jeffrey L. Rotman), **24** (Martin Harvey/Gallo Images), pp. **8**, **18**; Getty Images/Photodisc p. **25**; Harcourt Index/Digital Vision p. **5**; Heather Angel/Natural Visions pp. **7** (Norman T. Nicoll), p. **16**; Nature Picture Library pp. **12** (Jurgen Freund), **26** (Vincent Munier); NHPA pp. **11** (Pete Atkinson), **13** (Michael Patrick O'Neill), **22** (Daniel Heuclin); PA Photos p. **10**; SPL pp. **15** (Fred Winner/Jacana), **17** (Peter Scoones).

Cover photograph of a whale shark eating reproduced with permission of Bruce Coleman/Franco Banfi.

The Publishers would like to thank Michael Scott for his assistance in the preparation of this book.

Disclaimer
All Internet addresses (URLs) given in this book were valid at the time of going to press. However, due to the dynamic nature of the Internet, some addresses may have changed, or sites may have changed or ceased to exist since publication. While the author and Publishers regret any inconvenience this may cause readers, no responsibility for any such changes can be accepted by either the author or the Publishers.

Every effort has been made to contact copyright holders of any material reproduced in this book. Any omissions will be rectified in subsequent printings if notice is given to the Publishers.

Contents

Words in bold, **like this**, are explained in the Glossary.

What is an ocean food web?

All living things are **organisms**. Organisms are eaten by other organisms. Small animals get eaten by bigger animals, who get eaten by even larger animals. When large animals die they get eaten by tiny insects, maggots and **bacteria**. Even mighty killer whales die and rot and are eaten by bacteria and **bottom feeders**. If you draw lines between each of the animals, showing who eats whom, you create a diagram called a food web.

The organisms in ocean **habitats** are part of a food web. In food web diagrams, the arrows lead from the food to the animal that eats it.

This food web is from the Atlantic Ocean.

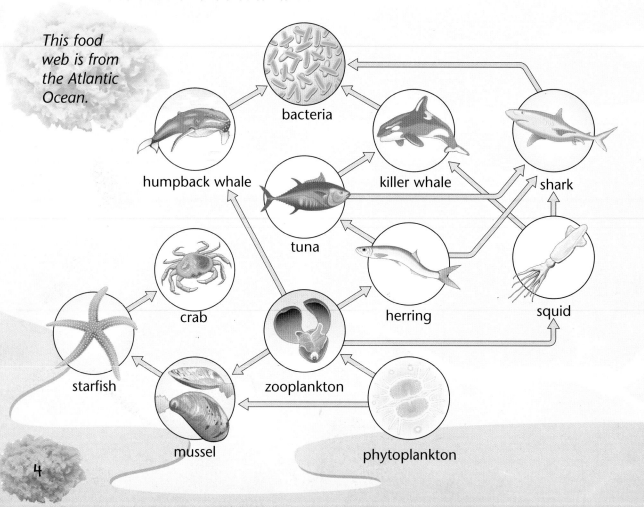

bacteria

humpback whale

killer whale

shark

tuna

crab

herring

squid

starfish

zooplankton

mussel

phytoplankton

What are ocean habitats like?

The oceans provide us with food, **minerals** and **energy**, and are important in controlling the Earth's **climate**. They are full of life. Particular plants and animals live in ocean habitats because they are especially suited or **adapted** to life there. They are part of the ocean food web because the plants or animals they feed on live in the ocean too.

There are two main ocean habitats for animals: out in the open water, or on the ocean floor. Most fish and sea **mammals** live in open waters, or in **coral reefs** or rocky coastal waters. Many other animals, such as crabs, snails and sea worms, live on the ocean floor. Some live in burrows in the mud or sand of the seabed. Most **species** live in the first 100 metres (about 330 feet) where sunlight can still reach into the water. In deeper water it becomes darker and colder and there is less life.

Coral reefs in the warm shallow waters of tropical oceans are home to thousands of animals.

What is an ocean food chain?

A food web looks quite complex. It is actually made up of lots of different food chains. Food chains are simpler diagrams. They show the way some of the animals in a food web feed on each other. The arrows in the chain show the movement of food and **energy** from plants to animals as they feed on each other.

Most **organisms** are part of more than one food chain because they eat more than one type of food. This is safer for them. An organism that eats only one type of food will not **survive** if that food runs out.

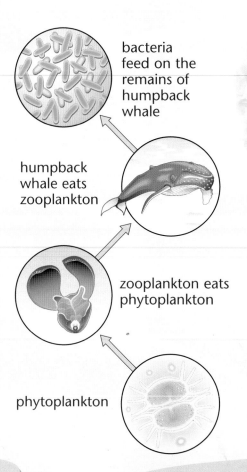

bacteria feed on the remains of humpback whale

humpback whale eats zooplankton

zooplankton eats phytoplankton

phytoplankton

This diagram of an ocean food chain shows how energy passes from one link in the chain to another.

Starting the chain

Most food chains start with the energy from the Sun. Plants such as **algae** trap the energy in sunlight and use it to make their own food. Seaweeds are large algae that look quite similar to plants on land. They have green, red or brown fronds like leaves and are anchored to rocks or to the seabed with strong roots. Seaweeds grow in shallow waters along shorelines, but not in deeper waters where there is almost no sunlight. There may seem to be no plant life at all in these deeper waters, but it is there.

Most plant life in the ocean is made up of **microscopic** plant-like organisms called **phytoplankton**. These drift around in the water near the sunny surface, taking energy from the Sun and growing in vast numbers. They are food for many other animals in the sea, which gain energy from them. These animals in turn are eaten by other animals. In this way energy flows through the food chain and through the **habitat**.

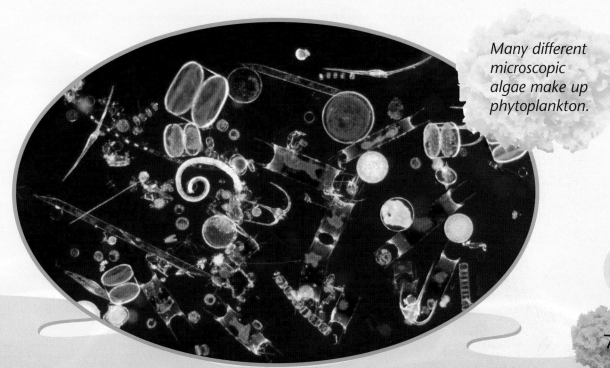

Many different microscopic algae make up phytoplankton.

7

Without sunlight, all the seaweeds and phytoplankton would die out. Phytoplankton produce more oxygen than all the plants on land. Without them, nearly all the organisms on our planet would die out.

Making the chain

Plants are called **producers**, because they trap the Sun's energy and produce food. Food chains usually start with producers. Animals are **consumers**. They have to eat other organisms to get energy. **Herbivores** are animals that eat plants. They are the **primary consumers** in a food chain. They often end up as food for meat-eating animals, called **carnivores**. In food chains we call these **secondary consumers**. Secondary consumers may also eat other secondary consumers, or scavenge (feed on) the remains of their **prey**. **Omnivores** eat plants as well as other animals. They are primary and secondary consumers.

Giant kelp is the largest type of seaweed. It grows in great 'forests' in some coastal areas. The biggest kelps can reach 30 metres (nearly 100 feet) tall.

More links in the chain

Food chains do not end with secondary consumers. All organisms eventually die. When they die their bodies are eaten by **scavengers** such as sea worms and **decomposers** such as bacteria. The waste from the decomposers sinks into the seabed and forms **nutrients**. When a **current** churns up the seabed the nutrients are swirled up towards the surface, where they can be **absorbed** by the phytoplankton. In this way the chain begins again.

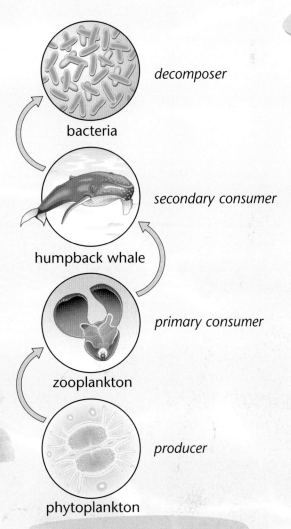

decomposer

bacteria

secondary consumer

humpback whale

primary consumer

zooplankton

producer

phytoplankton

This ocean food chain shows how energy moves from producer to primary consumer and then to secondary consumer and decomposer.

Breaking the chain

If some organisms in a food web die out, it may be disastrous for the others. **Environmental** change, such as a change in **climate** and sea temperature, can affect habitats.

Human activity, such as **pollution** from shipping, or industry, or overfishing animals like anchovy, tuna and whales, can cause breaks in ocean food chains and in natural cycles. Oceans and seas are often interlinked, so disturbing the food chain of one habitat can affect other ocean life thousands of kilometres away.

Japanese whalers catch a minke whale in the Southern Ocean. Massive overfishing led to a ban on commercial whaling in 1986, but Japan still catches whales for what it calls 'scientific purposes'.

Which producers live in oceans?

Plant-like **producers** called **phytoplankton** start ocean food chains. There are many **species** of phytoplankton, each with its own shape. Some are soft-bodied and can change shape.

Like plants on land, phytoplankton need sunlight, water and **nutrients** to grow. Phytoplankton stay mostly near the surface to catch the sunlight. **Currents** push nutrients up from the seabed to the surface, where they are **absorbed** by the phytoplankton. Phytoplankton are a vital source of food for many other **microscopic** animals and small fish. In summer they can grow in such vast quantities the sea starts to look like a reddish-brown soup. This is called a phytoplankton 'bloom' or a 'red tide'.

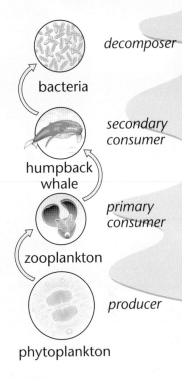

decomposer

bacteria

secondary consumer

humpback whale

primary consumer

zooplankton

producer

phytoplankton

'Red tides' like this are made up of billions of phytoplankton.

Seaweeds and other green plants like seagrasses and **algae** can be found nearer the shore in shallow waters. These plants are also essential food for small animals like sea urchins and big animals like dugongs and turtles.

Dugongs mainly live in shallow, tropical seas in Western Australia. Just like Florida's manatees, they feed mostly on seagrass and can grow to 3 metres (about 10 feet) long.

Breaking the chain: producers

Phytoplankton are essential to ocean food chains, but need certain conditions to grow. Currents of cold water containing nutrients rise up from the seabed, helping phytoplankton to grow. Some weather conditions make surface water warm. Warm water has already given up its nutrients, so there is no more food for the phytoplankton. As the phytoplankton starve, so too do the fish and **mammals** that eat them.

Which primary consumers live in oceans?

Primary consumers are plant-eating animals. **Phytoplankton** are the most important source of plant food in the ocean. They are mostly eaten by slightly larger **zooplankton**. Zooplankton is the name of a huge variety of tiny animals, some **microscopic**, others just a few centimetres long. They are all too small to swim against the ocean **currents**, and drift where the water takes them. Zooplankton usually include the **larvae** of larger animals such as fish, squid, **molluscs** and **crustaceans**. Zooplankton are eaten by **filter feeders**, small fish, shrimp and even whales!

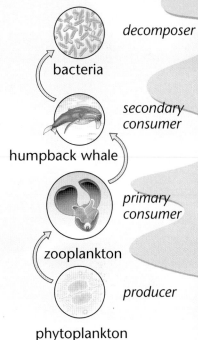

decomposer
bacteria

secondary consumer
humpback whale

primary consumer
zooplankton

producer
phytoplankton

*Sea slugs are molluscs that graze on seaweeds, so they are primary condumers. They are often brightly coloured. The colours warn **predators** that they have stinging cells on their backs.*

*Krill feed by filtering **algae** out of the water or scraping them off the sea ice. They in turn are food for a whole range of other animals.*

Krill

Among the most important zooplankton animals are krill. Krill are small, shrimp-like crustaceans found mostly in the Southern Ocean. They eat phytoplankton and are 1–6 centimetres (0.5 to 2.5 inches) long. Krill spend the day in deep waters, safe from most predators. At night they swim up to the surface waters to feed on phytoplankton.

A single krill can lay up to 10,000 eggs, several times a year. If there is plenty of phytoplankton to eat, krill numbers will also build up, turning the waters pink for many kilometres. The weight of krill in the Southern Ocean is estimated to reach 650 million tonnes (about 640 million tons) in the summer! Krill is one of the most plentiful animals on Earth. They are a vital source of food for many fish, squid and seabirds. Their largest predators are **baleen** whales.

Which secondary consumers live in oceans?

Nearly all sea animals die by being eaten by a **secondary consumer**. Secondary consumers can be small, like the barnacle, which waves its feather-like feet in the water to catch **zooplankton**. They can also be massive, like the blue whale, which uses its **baleen** plates to catch and eat krill.

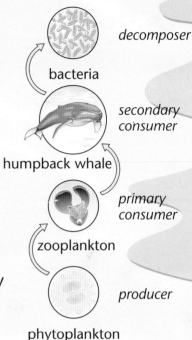

decomposer

bacteria

secondary consumer

humpback whale

primary consumer

zooplankton

producer

phytoplankton

Ocean predators

On the sea floor there are many animals specially designed to attack their chosen **prey**. Starfish wrap themselves around **molluscs** such as oysters, and pull their shells apart to eat the animal inside.

In open waters, the huge manta ray simply opens its vast mouth and filters zooplankton and tiny fish from the water. The huge black marlin, one of the fastest fish in the sea, powers through the surface waters chasing fast prey such as tuna, mackerel and squid.

A starfish puts its stomach inside a clam's shell and eats the clam while it is still in its shell.

Deep-sea predators

Deep in the ocean depths, secondary consumers have developed special ways of catching their prey. Many of the fish, squid and shrimp here have organs on their skin that can produce light. They use these lights to attract prey or to dazzle a **predator**. Female anglerfish use their light organ to attract smaller fish and squid.

The largest of all deep-sea predators is the sperm whale. They hunt squid, large fish, and even deep water sharks. Their favourite prey is the mysterious giant squid, which has been found dead on beaches but has never been seen alive.

The light organ on the nose of this deep-sea anglerfish attracts prey. Its huge mouth can open to swallow prey bigger than itself.

Which decomposers live in oceans?

Decomposers are the other major group in a food web. They feed on the remains of dead animals and plants, and their waste. **Bacteria** are ocean decomposers. They break down dead animals and plants into simpler substances, such as **nutrients**. **Phytoplankton** take in the nutrients this produces, and so the food chain starts all over again.

Animals that help decomposers

When animals die, other animals called **scavengers** eat them and break them down into smaller bits that decomposers can use. Scavengers may be **bottom feeders** like crabs and lobsters, or small fish and even sharks.

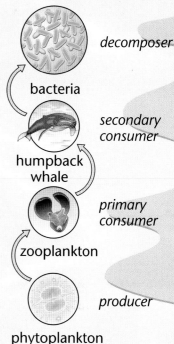

decomposer

bacteria

secondary consumer

humpback whale

primary consumer

zooplankton

producer

phytoplankton

A whale carcass will be fed upon by lots of scavengers. Some smaller scavengers, such as crabs and sea worms, may live on its remains for up to 50 years!

Sea cucumbers are strange tube-like scavengers that move slowly along the seabed. They shovel sand into their mouths with their feelers and suck out any decaying animal and plant matter from the sand.

Sea urchins feed by scooping **algae** into their mouths, with the shovel-like teeth under their bodies. They are covered in very sharp spines to protect them from **predators**. Sea urchins live on the ocean floor, and can move slowly on soft tube-like feet.

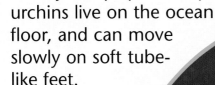

*Some sea cucumbers are brightly coloured and seem to be easy **prey** for fish, but they are often poisonous.*

How are ocean food chains different in different places?

Although oceans share many features, their food chains can be very different. They are affected by the **climate**, the **currents** and depth of the water, and by the life living near by. Human activity will also affect them.

The Southern Ocean

The Southern Ocean is the fourth longest ocean in the world. It surrounds the **continent** of Antarctica. Severe storms, strong winds, huge icebergs and sea ice are found here. The animals that live here are **adapted** for life in a harsh climate.

Many **species** of seal live here, including the fur seal and elephant seal. Seals were once over-hunted for their oil and skin, but they are now protected. Although seals spend a lot of time on land, they hunt in the sea for fish and krill.

Southern elephant seals are found throughout the Southern Ocean. They feed mainly on squid and fish.

One large **predator** in the Southern Ocean is the leopard seal. It has spotted fur, like a leopard, and is a fierce hunter. It eats krill but also hunts penguins, squid, fish and other seals. It can even jump out of the water to snatch penguins off the pack ice.

Several species of penguin live in the water and ice of the Southern Ocean. Chinstrap, macaroni and king penguins are all here, feeding on huge numbers of fish and krill.

Krill is the main source of food for many animals in the Southern Ocean. Some of the world's most **endangered** whales, such as the blue, fin, sei and humpback whales, come here in the summer to eat tonnes of krill.

This is a food chain from the Southern Ocean.

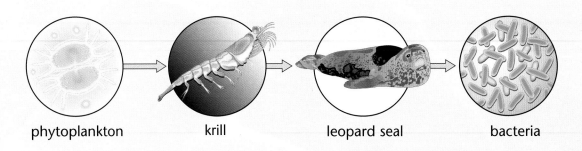

phytoplankton   krill   leopard seal   bacteria

The Pacific Ocean

The Great Barrier Reef is found in the Pacific Ocean, off the north-east coast of Australia. It contains the world's largest collection of **coral reefs**. Coral reefs are ideal **habitats** for many rare species. Small animals like sea snails move slowly over the coral feeding on **algae**. The coral itself is nibbled by smaller fish, or bitten off in big chunks by parrot-jawed trigger fish. Seagrasses provide food for green turtles and dugongs. Once the seagrasses die they begin to rot and are eaten by sea cucumbers, crabs and sea worms.

Large predators patrol the reefs looking for **prey**. Barracuda can grow up to 2 metres (6 feet) long and often hunt in packs. They open their mouths wide to bite large fish in half. The green turtle's only predator is the tiger shark, which eats anything, including rubbish!

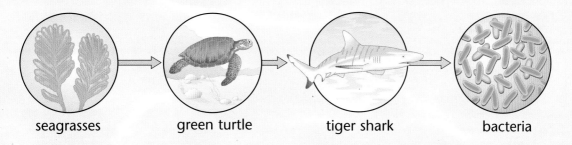

seagrasses   green turtle   tiger shark   bacteria

This is a food chain from the Great Barrier Reef. It includes the green turtle which is one of six species of marine turtle to be found in the Great Barrier Reef.

What happens to a food web when a food chain breaks down?

All around the world, ocean food chains and webs are under threat because of humans. Although much work is underway to stop further damage, these are some of the dangers currently faced by plants and animals in ocean **habitats**.

Pollution

One of the biggest threats to ocean food webs is from **pollution**. We pollute the oceans with waste from our homes, farms and factories. Pollution in the sea can also harm human life. Tiny plankton take in the poisons we put in seawater. When they are eaten by small fish and shellfish the poison passes along the food chain, until at some point an animal that has eaten poisons is caught and eaten by humans.

Rubbish thrown into the sea or on to beaches harms the environment and animals within it.

Industry

Oil and gravel occur naturally in oceans. When we take them from the seabed, we often disturb the places where new fish are born – and this reduces fish numbers. We may also pollute the oceans, especially with oil, which can cover the water for many kilometres. Oil can be washed on to coastal rocks where it kills beds of mussels and pollutes rock pools and beaches. Droplets of oil sink beneath the surface, where they poison sea life.

Sea birds like this penguin can get covered in oil from an oil slick. They become too heavy to fly, or die from poisoning as they try to clean their feathers.

Overfishing

Too much fishing of any **species** can upset the food chain. Over the last century, humans have overfished many species, so that numbers of herring, anchovy and cod have been drastically reduced. Although there are now some agreements in place to try to limit fishing, it is difficult to make sure they are being obeyed. Except for areas close to the coast, the ocean belongs to no country, so governments cannot do much to protect ocean life.

A bottlenosed dolphin swims near a drift net. These long nets are meant to catch tuna, but animals such as dolphins and sharks also get trapped in them and die.

Breaking the chain: how we are affected

When animals and plants are poisoned, killed or driven out of their habitat, it creates breaks in food chains and affects the entire food web of that area. Eventually, breaks or changes to food chains and webs affect us too. For example, in the Japanese town of Minamata in the last century thousands of people died or were injured as a result of mercury poisoning. They had eaten fish from the water polluted with mercury by the Chisso Corporation. The protection of ocean food webs is important for all living things.

How can we protect ocean food chains?

All around the world, scientists, governments and **environmental** groups are working to clean up and protect oceans and ocean food chains. They want to make sure that no further damage is done to these **habitats** and the animals and plants that depend on them.

International research and protection

Scientists make surveys of ocean habitats. They test water quality and **pollution** levels and they check animal and plant life to make sure that population levels are not falling. In this way scientists find the links in the food web that need protection.

Scientists tell governments how they can improve and protect ocean habitats. Governments around the world draw up agreements to try to protect fish stocks and prevent illegal fishing.

Much of this work has come too late for some **species**, but at least these agreements now give some protection from overfishing to species that provide food for many other animals.

An oil spill from the tanker Erika polluted this beach in Brittany, France in 1999. These volunteers are cleaning up and looking for seabirds covered in oil.

Campaigning groups

Environmental groups, like Friends of the Earth, Greenpeace and WWF, **campaign** to make sure that governments look after the oceans, by controlling pollution. Many countries are part of MARPOL, an international organization which works to protect coasts and seas from pollution from ships, oil and waste.

Conservation groups try to show people living near oceans how they can help to protect them, for everyone's future. All around the world, clean-up operations are trying to limit the damage to the environment caused by pollution. More than 130 countries are now part of the United Nations Environment Programme, with plans to tackle pollution in some of the world's dirtiest oceans.

Research an ocean food web

Although it takes special equipment to do deep ocean research, you can research habitats near the ocean. If you go to the seaside, think about the food chains there. Look in the rock pools and along the water's edge. Here are some suggestions to help you find out about animal and plant life.

1. What is the habitat like? Is it cold or warm, shady or light?
2. Can you see any plants or animals? Try to group them – which are the plants, insects, birds, fish and **crustaceans**?
3. What do you think each animal would like to eat?
4. Which are the **predators** and which are the **prey**?
5. Can you make a food chain of the animals and plants you see?
6. Think about how the habitat could change – how would change affect the wildlife there?

This beach in Cornwall, England is home to the hundreds of creatures that live in the rock pools and along the shoreline.

Where are the world's main oceans?

This map shows the location of the main oceans of the world. The Pacific Ocean is the largest, followed by the Atlantic, Indian and Southern Oceans. The Arctic Ocean is the smallest.

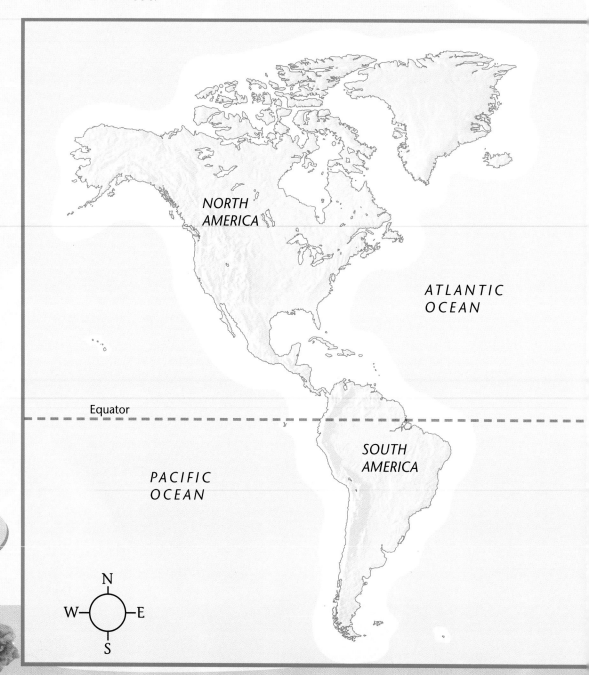

NORTH AMERICA

ATLANTIC OCEAN

Equator

SOUTH AMERICA

PACIFIC OCEAN

N
W — E
S

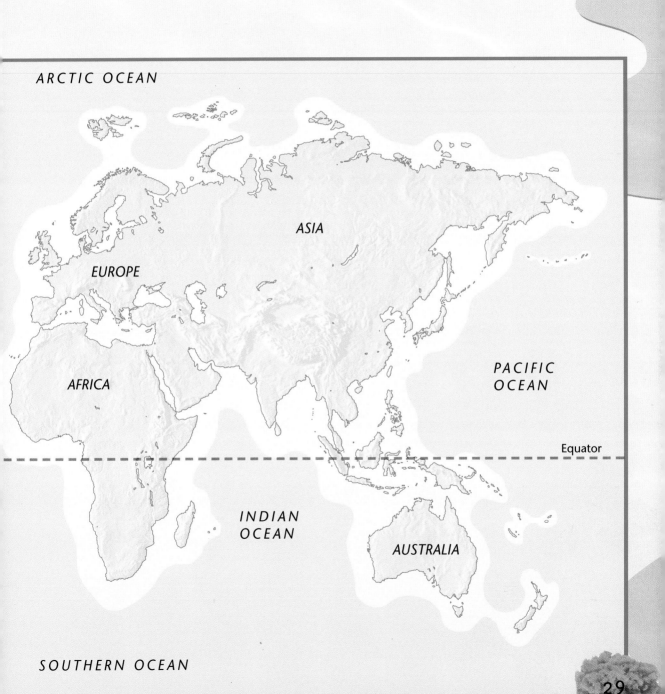

ARCTIC OCEAN

ASIA

EUROPE

AFRICA

PACIFIC
OCEAN

Equator

INDIAN
OCEAN

AUSTRALIA

SOUTHERN OCEAN

29

Glossary

absorb take in through the surface of skin, leaves or roots

adapted having special features that help an organism live in its habitat

algae (singular alga) small plant-like organisms

aquatic living in water

bacteria (singular bacterium) tiny living decomposers found everywhere

baleen hard layers on the upper jaw of some whales, used to filter plankton from the water

bottom feeders animals that feed on the seabed

campaign work to get something done or changed

carnivore animal that eats the flesh of another animal

climate the general conditions of weather in any area

conservation protecting and saving the natural environment

consumers organisms that eat other organisms

continent a land mass, such as Europe, Asia, Africa, N. America, S. America, Australia or Antartica

coral reef ridge of rocks formed from the skeletons of many tiny jelly-like animals

crustaceans hard-shelled animals that mainly live in water, such as crabs, lobsters and shrimps

current stream of water moving through part of the ocean

decomposers organisms that break down and get nutrients from dead plants and animals and their waste

endangered when a species of plant or animal is in danger of dying out completely

energy power to grow, move and do things

environment the surroundings in which an animal or plant lives, including the other animals and plants that live there

extinction the complete dying out of a species of animal or plant

filter feeders animals that eat by filtering tiny food particles from the water

habitat place where an organism lives

herbivore animal that eats plants

larvae (singular larva) the young of some insects and other animals

mammals group of animals that feed their babies on milk from their own bodies

microscopic too small to be seen without a microscope

minerals substances that occur naturally and are not made from plant or animal matter, for instance rocks or metals

molluscs soft-bodied animals, often with hard shells, such as snails, oysters and octopuses

nutrients substances that plants and animals need to live

omnivore animal that eats both plants and other animals

organism living thing

phytoplankton tiny, often microscopic plants and algae that float freely in the sea

pollution when chemicals or other substances that can damage animal or plant life escape into water, soil or the air

predators animals that hunt and eat other animals

prey animals that are caught and eaten by predators

primary consumers animals that eat plants

producer organism (plant) that can make its own food

scavengers organisms that feed on dead plants and animals, and waste

secondary consumer animal that eats primary consumers and other secondary consumers

species group of organisms that are similar to each other and can breed together to produce young

survive continue to live healthily

tentacles long, flexible feelers, used for feeling, moving or grasping

venom poison delivered by a sting or bite

zooplankton tiny, often microscopic animals that float in the sea

Find out more

Books and CD-Roms

Cycles in Nature: Food Chains, Theresa Greenaway (Hodder Wayland/Raintree Steck-Vaughn, 2001)

Science Answers: Food Chains and Webs, Louise and Richard Spilsbury, (Heinemann Library, 2004)

Taking Action: WWF, Louise Spilsbury (Heinemann Library, 2000)

Food Chains and Webs CD-ROM (Heinemann Library, 2004) has supporting interactive activities and video clips.

Websites

www.bbc.co.uk/nature/blueplanet/games.shtml
This site has games based on facts and articles from their sea life section.

Find out more about the conservation work of these organizations at:
www.wwf.org.uk   WWF-UK
www.wwf.org.au   WWF Australia
www.foe.co.uk   Friends of the Earth
www.foe.org.au   Friends of the Earth Australia
www.greenpeace.org.uk   Greenpeace

Index

Titles in the *Food Chains and Webs* series include:

Hardback   0 431 11903 1

Hardback   0 431 11905 8

Hardback   0 431 11904 X

Hardback   0 431 11902 3

Hardback   0 431 11901 5

Hardback   0 431 11900 7

Find out about the other titles in this series on our website www.heinemann.co.uk/library